25024

2.50

GRIEF AND BEREAVEMENT
Understanding Children

Ann Couldrick
Bereavement Service Manager
Sir Michael Sobell House
Churchill Hospital, Oxford

Illustrations by
Frankie McGauran
Volunteer
Sir Michael Sobell House
Churchill Hospital, Oxford

SOBELL PUBLICATIONS
Sir Michael Sobell House, Oxford

Grief and Bereavement: Understanding Children

©Sobell Publications
Sir Michael Sobell House
Churchill Hospital, Oxford

First published in 1988 by Sobell Publications
Reprinted 1989, 1991

ISBN 0 9517537 1 1

Printed in Great Britain by
DS Litho, Bicester, Oxon

PREFACE

The death of a parent is an overwhelming experience and it can be particularly difficult to understand the reactions and responses of children because children react according to their age and maturity.

Children experience the pain of loss as intensely as adults, their world has been overturned too. This booklet may help you to understand some of the ways children respond to grief and how you can help your child. You are not alone; others are facing the same difficulties and you can contact them through CRUSE, the national organization offering support to all who are bereaved. (See appendix)

In Britain, there are many children under 16 who have lost a parent through death. Although you may fear for the psychological well-being of your child, there is plenty of evidence that children are not necessarily damaged by the experience, and indeed may grow stronger.

How may I help my child? ......

You might like to think about the following:

Your children need information

Your children need to see that you are grieving

Your children need extra affection

Thinking about what has happened ......

Be clear and honest. Despite your instinct to protect, information that is <u>not</u> truthful and realistic is harmful. Communicate in words and ways he can understand given his age and abilities. Check back that he has understood your words and make time for the questions he needs to ask over and over again.

The following half truths are not helpful and may be misinterpreted as follows:

o   *"Mummy has gone away"*
     Child's reaction - "Why didn't she take me? I must have been bad to make her leave me"

o   *"God took Mummy because she was so good"*
     Child's reaction - anger against God "I needed her" - fear of being good "I might be taken"

o   *"Daddy is sleeping forever"*
     Child's reaction - fear of going to sleep.

You or someone close to the child should tell him what has happened, preferably at home where he feels safe. Be specific, very young children are not able to understand that death is irreversible, but they can understand the analogy of death being like a broken toy. The dead person cannot be mended and although we want to, we cannot put it right. Explain that his parent's body has stopped working and it will not do the things it used to do like walking, talking, moving or breathing. Tell your child that the dead person does not feel anything any longer, is not sad, is not hurting, feeling cold or feeling ill. This is important because it is hard to understand burial or cremation if he does not have this information.

Repeated questions ......

Recognize that these may occur for many months after the death and are not as much for factual information as they are for reassurance that the story has not changed. Your child is checking to make sure that things are still the same and that what happened is still true, just as you may wish that what has taken place is only a bad dream from which you will wake up.

2

Reassurance ......

The need for reassurance that he is still loved and precious is important; your child needs to know that he will be cared for as long as he needs it even though such a sad thing has happened; that his physical needs will be met and that you know that he is sad and upset.

Show your grief ......

This allows your child to express his. Make sure he knows these feelings are normal and will not last forever. Let him know you are going to tell him what is happening, that he is part of the family and that all of you will get through this together. This will develop secure feelings again and allow him to trust you although his world has changed. Spend as much time as you can with your child, give affection and show your support physically, really look at him and touch him frequently, he desperately needs the reassurance this gives.

Funeral rituals ......

You may feel you want to protect your child from this very sad occasion. Your child however, needs to understand what is happening. Many bereaved children looking back, have expressed sadness and anger that they were excluded. If he decides that he wants to attend, the whole of the service should be explained so that he has some idea of what to expect. Of course he will be sad, but you are giving him an opportunity to say goodbye. You are preparing him for dealing with real life, and you will be there to support and be supported by him. If he decides not to accompany you, then his decision should be respected. You can tell him that he can visit the grave or the church whenever he feels ready. Never force a child to do something he does not want to.

One father took his three year old daughter to say goodbye to her mother in the hospital Chapel. She hesitated at the door, holding her father's hand, she looked at her mother from the door and said "I don't want to go in, my Mummy has gone". He held her close and they both blew a kiss. He explained the funeral to her and she decided to go to nursery school. Instead, half way through the afternoon session, she suddenly decided that she needed to be with her daddy and the teacher brought her to the church just as the coffin was being lowered into the grave. She stood quietly by her father holding tightly to his hand. He was greatly comforted by her presence.

Understanding your child's behaviour ......

It is important to try to enter your child's own world.

A child grieves like an adult ......

But he expresses his grief in different ways. Because of his emotional immaturity, he does not have the thinking abilities to make sense of it. He tends not to have the words to describe his feelings, thoughts and memories. Therefore, his behaviour is your guide. Is he irritable over every little setback? Does he burst into tears every time he is thwarted? It might help to think of his grief as a deep river, flowing beneath the surface of his life, and like a river, every now and then the pressure becomes intolerable and bursts through the surface. This behaviour is very hard for you to bear because you probably feel the same way. If you can, hold him, comfort him, just as you would like to be comforted yourself. Gradually this tempestuous behaviour will settle down, although it may still recur from time to time.

Grandparents, where available, can be a great comfort and provide stability for the family. Sometimes, however, they may so badly want to protect themselves from the child's pain that they will deny that the child has taken in what has happened, or that the child is capable of grief.

Some children contain their pain for a very long time, perhaps unconsciously because they sense that you simply cannot help them yet. They become very quiet and "good". Try and help them to open up and to share those feelings. Reminisce together, re-visit favourite places that remind you of happier times and talk about the mum or dad who is not able to be with you. Grieving is very hard work. It takes time and energy so do not forget you both need treats occasionally.

The family pet can be a very real solace, their undemanding acceptance of the child can be very comforting.

Do not be surprised at their ability to "put it down". Children cannot get into a car and drive to a friend for solace, or pick up the phone - they are trapped with their feelings. Unlike adults, they do not have the capacity to tolerate intense pain over a long time. This is why your child may manifest grief intermittently as he alternately approaches and avoids his feelings so do not be surprised at this behaviour.

o   An eight year old boy came home from his father's funeral, put on his tracksuit and ran up to the local park to play football with his friends. He was not being heartless, he needed a break.

o   Richard was 12 when his mother died in a motor car accident. After he was told, he said quietly, "I'd better make some sandwiches, there will be lots of visitors". Six months later he began to be rude, defensive and difficult. It took this length of time for him to feel that his world was safe enough to express his feelings.

Play ......

A child's play is his work. Play is the natural means of communication for a child. It enables him to express himself and to release anxiety about events over which he has no control.

o   After her father died in a helicopter crash, Judith, aged three years, had a favourite game which lasted for many weeks. She would stand on the edge of her sandpit and direct her friends to drop their toys in the sand, then she firmly stamped them in. In this way she was making real within her, an event that had taken place outside.

If you can, give your child opportunities to draw and this will enable him to reveal what is going on in his inner world. Ask him to draw the family, perhaps doing something together. Encourage him by asking him to tell you about his picture.

o   Edward, aged six, repeatedly drew a long yellow rocket with a little boy sitting astride, it pointed at a sun on top of which was a matchstick Mummy. His inner wish was quite clear although he could not put it into words.

Different ages and some expected responses ......

The infant up to 1 year

Good consistent nurturing will meet his needs. That is - regular feeds, cuddles and comfort. A baby is able to accept care from anyone, although it is better if given by the same person and he may be restless and fretful whilst he adjusts to the change.

1 year - 2 years

A small child will be shocked by the sudden disappearance of someone he depends upon. He will show his distress about this and may cry every time he is not held and cry more at bed time. He may become sad and subdued and disinterested in his surroundings. A child cannot tolerate these feelings for very long and will eventually turn to someone else who can provide for his needs. Like the infant, consistent substitute parenting will help him.   •

2 years - 5 years

At this age a child cannot fully understand the permanence of death. He will search for the missing parent and ask the same questions over and over again. His anger may display itself in tantrums, aggressive and destructive behaviour. Knowing that he is expressing his grief in his way may help you to be patient and consoling.

The loss can be made worse by sending the child away to an unfamiliar environment in an attempt to protect him. It is better for him to be with his family; his routine needs to be maintained as much as possible.

He will need more physical contact even though he may be so angry and destructive. When a small child loses a parent he may regress, that is become more of a baby than he was before. You may be urging him to be a "Big Boy" when really he is trying to return to a time of safety and security. Physically this may show itself by becoming wet and soiled, needing feeding and needing babying. This loss of safety and security may make him more vulnerable to infection and he may have many more coughs and colds than usual. Bear with it, he is helpless to change his behaviour and it will pass if you and others can try to meet his needs.

Any new change will be difficult.

Starting school

This may become a battle. Remember, he is no longer sure that you will be there when he comes home. Be steadfast, enlist the teacher's help. Shorten his day at school if possible, and always be where you said you would.

Remember it will pass. Do not forget that many children who have not been bereaved find attending school difficult.

5 - 11 years old

At this age your child understands more about death and its implications, although not at an adult level. Denial is often his prime defence. He may act as though nothing has happened. Because of this you may unconsciously withdraw your support. He needs his inner deep feelings acknowledged. It may help him to reminisce with you, to see you grieve, to have keepsakes and photographs to help his suppressed feelings emerge.

He may feel guilt and will need reassurance that his behaviour did not cause the death. Give him permission to talk about his dead parent with you, with his friends and with his teacher. Just knowing that he is not the only child in this position can help.

Making time to talk about past holidays and shared times can help you to share feelings with each other. This will help you both understand the other's experience.

Adolescence

The adolescent feels very much like an adult in his response to death but these feelings may be complicated by the problems of adolescence. Trying to become adult and stand on his own feet is difficult enough and he will be torn between this and needing you as he did as a child. His relationship with you may have been stormy before the illness and death intervened, and guilt that his behaviour contributed to the death can complicate his feelings of loss. He may even have wished the illness was over and feel terrible guilt about those thoughts. It may help to reassure him that many people also feel like that when someone they love is dying. He may contain his grief until he finds someone he can trust among his friends or someone nearer his own age.

It is better that the young person should not be expected to take on the responsibilities of the dead parent. Although he needs to know what is happening, try not to burden him with the difficulties you are facing but at the same time include him, consult him, respect his feelings and reassure him. Older children are often very resourceful however, so encourage him if he wants to try and help.

This is also the time to reinforce some clear family rules. Because you are distracted, it is very easy for the older child to think that you do not care where he is or when he comes home. Make it clear that he matters even more to you than before. If you have a friend or an adult family member of the same sex as your child, that you trust, encourage them to come close. This will give your son or daughter a role model and another shoulder to lean on.

Who else can I turn to for advice or help? ......

1.   Your family doctor and health visitor will understand what you are going through as a family and can introduce you to other organizations who might help.

2.   If your child is of school age, it will be helpful to keep in contact with his school teacher. After all, half his waking day will be at school. A sympathetic teacher can be a real resource and can keep you in touch with his learning progress.

It is not unusual for children to appear to stop making progress during the time they are adjusting to a great loss and it will help your child if you keep in touch. This will make it easier for the school to alert you to any upset behaviour and thus perhaps avert serious problems.

3.   The Child Guidance Clinic can offer advice and support to families who are encountering problems with behaviour. Referral can be made by you, your family doctor, or the school.

4.   The Social Services - available in every town, may be able to offer practical support.

You and your needs ......

    You are bereaved too. This means that you will be acutely grieving at the same time as you are trying to help your child.

o   You can only do your best, one day at a time.

o   Be realistic about what you can expect from yourself.

o   Tap other resources for help for your child and yourself.

o   If you have a bad day put it behind you and have another go.

o   Understand and accept the loss of energy, emotional and physical, and try and care for yourself as well.

o   You will need to get away from the family at times, even though you know they need you. This is healthy selfishness. To survive the huge task of mourning, you have to care for yourself the way the best mother in the world would care for you. Put your guilt down occasionally because you cannot meet all the needs of your child. Remember, he has resources of his own and eventually you will both have been strengthened by the experience in a way that other people who have not been through this, will never be.

o   Do not despair, we need you and your experience.

o   Believe in yourself and believe in the future, both for you and your family.

Books you might like to read with your children:

For young children:

Badger's Parting Gifts
S Varley

Kirsty's Kite
CC Stilz

Why did Grandma Die?
T Madler

Water Bugs and Dragonflies
D Stickney

Grandpa and Me
M & B Alex

The Tenth Good Thing About
Barney
J Voirst

For older children to read:

A Taste of Blackberries
D Buchanan Smith

How it Feels when a Parent
Dies
J Krementz

Your Friend Rebecca
L Hoy

Mama's Going to Buy You a
Mocking Bird
J Little

A Sound of Chariots
M Hunter

A Star for the Latecomer
B & P Zindel

The Little Prince
Antoine de Saint-Exupery

Books that you might like to read:

In the Midst of Winter
MK Moffatt

Helping Children Cope with Grief
R Wells

Explaining Death to Children
E Grollman

Helping Children Cope with
Separation and Loss
C Jewitt

The Courage to Grieve
J Tatelbaum

When People Die
G Williams & J Ross

There are many other books in the bookshops. If you find one or more that are really helpful, we would love to hear from you so that we may improve our service.

Please write to: Mrs Ann Couldrick
                          Sir Michael Sobell House
                          Churchill Hospital, Oxford

Bibliography:

How it Feels When a Parent Dies, Kermentz J
Victor Gallancz Ltd 1986

Grieving, Rando T
Lexington Books 1988

Studies of Grief in Adult Life, Parkes CM
Penguin Books 1975

You may also find the following organizations to be helpful:

CRUSE   The National Organization for Widows, Widowers and their Children

National Address: Local Address:

CRUSE House   CRUSE Bereavement Care
126 Sheen Road   Wesley Memorial Hall
Richmond   New Inn Hall Street
Surrey TW9 1UR   Oxford

Tel: 081 940 4818/9047   Tel: Oxford 245398

PARENTLINE

Wesley Memorial Hall
New Inn Hall Street
Oxford   Tel: Oxford 726600

SAMARITANS

123 Iffley Road
Oxford   Tel: Oxford 722122

Further copies of this booklet may be obtained from:

The Study Centre Coordinator
Sir Michael Sobell House
Churchill Hospital, Oxford OX3 7LJ